LOVEKNOTS
to
LARIATS

LOVEKNOTS
to
LARIATS

Ramona Cugnini

iUniverse LLC
Bloomington

LOVEKNOTS TO LARIATS

iUniverse books may be ordered through booksellers or by contacting:

iUniverse LLC
1663 Liberty Drive
Bloomington, IN 47403
www.iuniverse.com
1-800-Authors (1-800-288-4677)

ISBN: 978-1-4917-2051-6 (sc)
ISBN: 978-1-4917-2049-3 (hc)
ISBN: 978-1-4917-2050-9 (e)

Library of Congress Control Number: 2014901180

Printed in the United States of America.

iUniverse rev. date: 02/27/2014

Cover by Steve Harris

CONTENTS

LOVE 1
    THE DOOR TO MY HEART 3
    A LESSON LEARNED 4
    THE KNOWLEDGE OF LOVE 5
    CHALICE OF LOVE 6
    GOING, GOING, GONE 7
    ILL-FITTING HALOS 8
    IF YOU DANCE 9
    KEEPSAKES 10
    LET EACH ACHIEVE HIS OWN 11
    LET'S SAY KING'S X 12
    MOUNTAIN LOVE 13
    MY GIFT FROM GOD 14
    MY FANTASY 15
    THE GAMBLE 16
    WORLD GROWING DIM 17
    GUILTY 18
    MOVING SALE 19
    THE MANY SHADES OF LOVE 20

LIFE 21
    A HAPPY HEART 23
    TRAVEL HOPEFULLY 24
    APRIL 15TH 25
    SOWING SEEDS 26
    A YEAR 27
    THE GRAVEYARD OF MY DREAMS 28
    MY FIRST DAY OF SCHOOL 29
    MARVEL 30
    HOW LONG IS A MONTH? 31

I AM MY BROTHER'S KEEPER..33

EVERYBODY'S GOTTA BE SOMEWHERE 34

BOWLING...35

THE SONG OF THE ANTIQUE COLLECTOR 36

THE SIGN READS "SOLD" 37

CLOUDS 38

TODAY 39

THE ODE TO THE FISHERMAN 40

HIGH-MINDED DREAMER 41

MY HOPES 42

IF I WERE A BREEZE 43

OUR COUNTRY 44

WHAT MAKES A MAN 45

UPON REACHING SIXTY-TWO 46

THE APPLE DOESN'T FALL FAR FROM THE TREE.....................47

AN "OLD ADAGE" STORY 48

ALL OF ONE SIZE...50

A MODERN DAY "SANTA" MOM..51

A FAIRY TALE 52

GO FOR THE GOOD TIMES 53

DON'T MAKE ME COME DOWN THERE.......................................54

LEGENDS **55**

A TENDERFOOT AT MESA VERDE..57

THE WHISTLE SPEAKS 58

THE CLIFF DWELLER'S HOME 59

THE TRAIN RIDE...60

MESA VERDE 61

LYRICS..**63**

VICTIM...65

THE RICH MAN'S TABLE..66

WHY COULDN'T THAT BE ME 67

MYSTIC MOUNTAIN 68

LIGHTER SIDE **69**

"THE OLD WOMEN WHO LIVED IN A SHOE" 71

"LITTLE JACK HORNER" 72

"BO PEEP" 73

"LITTLE BOY BLUE" 74

"HUMPTY DUMPTY" 75

THE THREE LITTLE KITTENS...76

"SING A SONG OF SIXPENSE" 78

THE VILLAGE IDIOT 79

"DING DONG BELL" 80

LARIATS **81**

COWBOY HEROES..83

HOW THE COWBOY HAS CHANGED 84

THE RANCHER MEETS GOD 86

THE OLD BUCKBOARD...87

MY CHOSEN PIECE OF LAND 89

THE TEAM ROPER'S WIFE 90

A PIECE OF HIS HIDE..92

THE BARREL RACER..94

COWPOKE POKER...95

COUNTRY DANCES...96

A MOTHER COW—A RANCHERS FRIEND 97

A MESSAGE TO THE BRIDE 98

WHAT I REMEMBER 100

MY WIFE..101

PROFESSOR JOHN..102

FEEDLOT CATTLE 103

GOD'S MASTERPIECE 104

HOW THE COWBOY STANDS 105

A LEGEND IN HIS TIME 106

MY DADDY'S STETSON HAT... 108

MY MAMMA 109

DEDICATION

To my sister, Avis Harris
***
This book is dedicated to my sister Avis.

AVIS

*The look of keen intelligence
Is shining in her eyes.
Concern for poor unfortunates,
Whom lessor souls despise.*

*Where kindness and compassion
Enhance her natural grace,
And a happy sense of humor
Lights up her pretty face.*

*With a soul that cries for freedom
That no heavy chains can hold,
And a spirit of eternal youth,
That years cannot make old.*

*A kind, warm-hearted person,
With no taint of prejudice . . .
A blessing to this troubled earth,
I'm proud to call her "SIS".*

*A special thank you to my nephew. Steve Harris of Durango,
Colorado for his drawing of the book's cover.*

LOVE

THE DOOR TO MY HEART

I opened the door to my heart
And eagerly bade you come in.
You scorned my sincere invitation
And mocked with a taunting grin.

In anguish I pleaded and begged
As you turned and strode briskly away.
Still the door was left hopefully open,
By chance you'd return there some day.

I anxiously waited and wondered
And hoped for your knock at the door.
'Til at last in my dark desperation
I closed it to open no more.

Now I hear you incessantly rapping
As you call me again and again,
But the door once so eagerly opened
Is bolted and locked from within.

A LESSON LEARNED

When I was young I used to think
Someday I'd drape myself in mink.
Though, then I dressed in gingham gowns,
And other peoples hand-me-downs.

I dreamed my ship would soon come in,
Some years passed by, then numbered ten.
Good fortune did not come my way,
I toiled in vain for little pay.

And then I knew all in a flash,
Life's treasures can't be bought with cash.
The furs, the jewels and limousine,
Was nothing but a shallow dream.

I realized that all this time,
Far greater treasures had been mine.
For you've been here for many years,
To hold my hand and dry my tears.

A lesson I have sorely learned,
A meager wage, that's proudly earned,
A true love when you're growing old,
Far over shadows all the gold.

THE KNOWLEDGE OF LOVE

I don't know if an "inkling" is made to hold ink,
Or which is the "Tiddley" and which is the "Wink",
Or what makes the blue in the sky up above,
But I know the comfort of God's endless love.

I don't know a verb from an adverb or noun,
Or how flies walk the ceiling and never fall down.
There are so many things I do not comprehend,
But I know the joy of a true loyal friend.

I don't know how a boomerang thrown, can return,
And many's the answer that I'll never learn,
But as I count my blessings I know to be glad,
For the undying love of my mother and dad.

The one simple fact you must not overlook,
There's so much in life you don't learn from a book.
You may not know fame, or have knowledge to boast,
But if you've known a true love, then you've known the most.

CHALICE OF LOVE

With silver mounted bridle bit,
And conchos shining bright,
With silver tapaderos
And his six guns fastened tight.

Upon a prancing stallion
With wicked flashing eyes,
He rode into my lonely life
And claimed me for his prize.

He gave me golden bracelets,
A snow white turtle dove,
And bade me sip the nectar
From his chalice of love.

Then with spurs a-jingle
He rode into the night,
And took the golden nectar
That filled me with delight.

Sweet nectar that I tasted
From a chalice offered me,
Will evermore be cherished
In my fondest memory.

GOING, GOING, GONE

There was a time when love was new,
Our joys were great, our needs were few.
We had so much to build upon,
But now I'm going, going, gone.

I tried to show my love for you,
Did everything you'd want me to.
Now there's no need of hanging on,
I'll soon be going, going, gone.

Where I am bound I just don't know.
I should have left you long ago,
So with the coming of the dawn,
I will be going, going, gone.

I'll dry my tears, no need to grieve.
You'll never find me once I leave,
So search from Maine to Oregon,
I will be going, going, gone.

ILL-FITTING HALOS

When you slip away to meet me,
And your velvet eyes entreat me
Not to tempt you to a shameless way of life.
Still my eager arms must hold you,
In their warmth I must enfold you,
And ensnare us in the tangled web of life.

Though the world may well malign us,
Must our past mistakes confine us?
Must our lips refuse the taste of summer wine?
As the burning flame consumes us,
Must the evil fate that dooms us
Leave the fruit of love to wither on the vine?

But so many things remind us
Of the heavy chains that bind us,
And the tilted, tarnished halos that we wear.
Halos that will never fit us,
Still their presence won't permit us
To betray the trust of those who place them there.

IF YOU DANCE

If you dance, you pay the fiddler.
Is a truth as old as time.
If you want to eat your piece of cake,
You must give up your dime.

If you dance, you pay the fiddler.
Everything must have it's price.
If a true love you would marry,
Then you must expect the rice.

If you dance, you pay the fiddler.
Fickle love's not here to stay.
I have loved and I have lost you,
Now the fiddler wants his pay.

KEEPSAKES

Mem'ries of the past unfold.
The love a gypsy once foretold,
As in my treasures I behold
A pair of earrings made of gold.

A wine glass from our favorite place,
A picture of your smiling face,
A dainty fan, bedecked with lace,
Mem'ries time cannot erase.

A teddy bear you won for me,
A figurine of ebony,
The music from a symphony,
Is all I have to comfort me.

Now that you're gone so far away,
I see my cherished dreams decay,
My broken heart is on display
Midst trinkets in a bright array.

LET EACH ACHIEVE HIS OWN

Why do the eyes of those who love
View us as angels from above,
Transforming us from mortal men,
Demanding perfect discipline,
And place a halo on our head,
And give us misty wings to spread?

For man is fashioned out of clay,
And cannot walk the righteous way.
Perfection is not his to gain
Nor heights of angels to attain.

Don't chart for him the narrow course
And try to keep him there by force.
For sometimes he is led astray
By life's enticing, bright bouquet.

But let the choice he makes be his,
And love him for the man he is.
And chances are, there'll come a day
To prove he did not lose the way.
You'll cheer to see him reach his throne,
And know he made it on his own!

LET'S SAY KING'S X

I played the game of love with you, and let you make the rules.
To play a game you cannot win is only done by fools.
Now I know who the loser is, and who is gonna win,
Let's say King's X, and start all over again.

For once I'd like to call your bluff, and see the cards you hold.
I'd like to know the things you do, the things you leave untold.
I know some day you're gonna lose . . . though I cannot say when,
Let's say King's X, and start all over again.

I think by now I've learned enough to get an even shake.
I've seen you play your game so long, and break the rules you make,
So ante up, and deal the cards and put your money in.
Let's play for keeps, this time I'm gonna win!

MOUNTAIN LOVE

Where the white, majestic mountains
Overlook the rippling stream,
I have found the one I've searched for,
I have found my priceless dream.

We watched the moon beams on the water,
Heard the eagle's lonely cry,
Laughed and loved there in the darkness,
Softly said our sad good-bye.

Where the white, majestic mountains,
Tower above the dense, dark pine,
Awaits the one who has my promise,
I'll return and make her mine.

We'll stroll once more beside the water,
Pick the wild flowers for her hair,
While the white, majestic mountains
Protect the love that's blooming there.

MY GIFT FROM GOD

God created the Heavens and Earth.
Before the first sunrises,
He saved a scrap of velvet brown
To make your smiling eyes.

Then God said, "Let there be light,"
And the darkness did depart,
And he put aside a tiny beam,
To shine from a tender heart.

Then he made the dazzling sun,
In the span of a little while,
And he saved a part of his masterpiece
To make your sunny smile.

Then He made the twinkling stars,
That light the midnight skies,
Knowing no mortal man would miss
Those shining in your eyes.

Then God saw that his work was good,
As he gazed from his throne above,
And sent you straight into my arms,
To light my life with love.

MY FANTASY

My love's a hopeless fantasy,
By way of explanation,
It never did exist, except
In my imagination.

You never gave me cause to hope.
I cannot say you lied,
I'm certain you were unaware
Of dreams I held inside.

'Tho shattered hopes surround me
In my ruined dreams I know,
A falsehood can become a truth
For wishing makes it so.

My love's a hopeless fantasy
Of my imagination,
But now I see it as it is—
The truth: In revelation.

THE GAMBLE

I sit down at the table and ask to be dealt in.
I draw the cards I need, and then I make my bet to win.
You raise my bet and make your bluff, and gather up the gold.
Again I am the loser, never seeing what you hold.

You say you're holding aces; that you drew them back to back,
I don't know how you got them; I just feel the deck is stacked.
Again I am the loser in your game that has no rules,
I know you play it often, with many other fools.

So gather up your aces, get the one that's up your sleeve,
I'm going to quit your cheating game; I'm making plans to leave.

WORLD GROWING DIM

The cold wintery winds whip the snow from the bough
Of the pine's swaying limb.

My back to the gale, I trudge on through the storm
In my world growing dim.

The snowflakes that fall on my cheeks turn to ice,
Like the kisses you gave in my fool's paradise.

I scoop up the snow, that lies deep in the drifts
Of my bleak, lonely land.

And fashion a ball like you molded my life
In the palm of your hand.

The cold icy snowdrifts loom threatening and grim,
As I walk all alone in my world growing dim.

I wait for the time when the sun melts the snow
And the flowers bloom bright.

For spring follows winter, and tears turn to laughter,
As day follows night.

But the wind's frozen voice seems to echo a hymn,
As I walk all alone in my world growing dim.

GUILTY

Retracing the footsteps that led me away
From a gay cottage door,
Whose walls rang with laughter, where love filled the room,
It's a sad, solemn story, reflecting my doom.

The storm battered door hangs loose on it's hinge
As the cold wind sweeps through.
The roof of the porch weighs so heavily it's pillars droop;
The floors creaking boards sadly calling for you.

The wind whips the sand of the bleak barren yard
Where the grass once grew green,
And windows of boards sternly gaze as I wait.
The walls echo, "Guilty," condemned to my fate!

The dust covered chairs stand empty and gray
As in silent reproach.
The table of oak reveals my disgrace,
A cover of cobweb supplanting its lace.

The trailing green vine creeping high on the wall
Stands withered and dead.
And threads of bright tinsel around it entwine,
Ensnared in the web of a spider's design.

The wind whips the sand of the bleak barren yard
Where the grass once grew green,
And windows of boards sternly gaze as I wait.
The walls echo, "Guilty," condemned to my fate!

MOVING SALE

Please put me through to 'Classified,'
I'd like to place an ad.
There's going to be a moving sale,
On Lonely Street near Sad.

I have some old fond memories,
From which I'd like to part.
Some shattered hopes, and faded dreams,
And slightly broken heart.

Please put me through to 'Classified',
Please set the type in 'Bold,'
And capitalize my 'Broken Heart,'
And run the ad 'til sold.

These things I have to offer
Are colored mostly blue,
As through the many lonely days,
They've lost their rosy hue.

So put me through to 'Classified,'
I'd like to place an ad,
And you can reach me anytime,
On Lonely Street, near Sad.

Ramona Cugnini

THE MANY SHADES OF LOVE

I hold within this heart of mine
A mural etched in love's design.
Resplendent love, forever true,
Once cast my world with rosy hue.

Love's masterpiece, however great,
Is often doomed by jealous fate.
And parting starts the tears anew
To fade the golden, rosy hue.

Oh, lonely time, my dreams suppress,
And veil them in forgetfulness.
Nor buried memories renew
To tint my world with shades of blue.

Take up thy brush, oh endless time,
Restore the love that once was mine.
Cast out the many shades of blue,
And paint my world with rosy hue.

LIFE

A HAPPY HEART

As dancing eyes reflect a happy heart,
I see the imp of mischief hiding there.
They may turn liquid blue and brim with tears,
Or icy blue—when temper starts to flare.

So many thoughts are shinning in those eyes,
Thoughts that words alone could not impart,
And I fancy that I hear the angels sing
When dancing eyes reflect a happy heart.

Ramona Cugnini

TRAVEL HOPEFULLY

When I was very young I vowed
That I'd pursue each silver cloud.
I'd chase each rainbow bright and bold
To claim my hidden pot of gold.

Some treasure just beyond my reach,
A mountain high, a sandy beach,
A bright and shining star above,
A rendezvous: Eternal love.

Then as the years went by, I learned
The things for which I often yearned,
When held secure within my scope,
Were something less than I had hoped.

The spoils of a gallant fight
Became a useless bauble bright.
Some true love I had sought and won,
Was never worth the distance run.

So chase the sunbeam's golden ray,
Pursuing dreams from day to day.
To keep enduring joy alive,
Travel with hope, but don't arrive.

APRIL 15TH

The accountant said, "Soon your tax will be due.
The forms are all finished, I'll send them to you."
The tax forms arrived brought by Federal Express,
Did they owe more than last year, or did they owe less?

They looked at those figures in shocked disbelief.
They thought they'd been robbed at the hands of a thief.
She said, "At this rate, we're bound to go bust,
I don't like sending money to those I don't trust."

He said, "This tax bill is downright absurd!
Guess I must sell the cows I had kept for the herd.
Old Roany might sell, he's the best of the lot,
But prob'ly for less than when he was bought."

Just maybe the banker will float us a loan,
And we won't have to sell all the assets we own.
We are playing a game that we'll never win,
When the bank is paid off, then it's tax time again!

SOWING SEEDS

I want to sow seeds of friendship and trust
For a bountiful harvest, ere I'm turned to dust.
I want to sow seeds of brotherly love,
That all may have hope, and the peace of a dove.

I want to sow seeds to harvest someday,
Of joy and compassion, and faith in the day.
And I want my garden to flourish and thrive,
I'll weed out despair, distrust and deprive.

When comes the harvest if I'm fast asleep,
I hope I've sown pleasure that others may reap.

A YEAR

A year is but a span of time, just twelve short months in all.
The seasons come, the seasons go, as winter follows fall.

A year may be so short a time, it's here, then gone again.
A fleeting moment of one's life, you hardly know it's been.

A year may be forever when your love is far away.
When empty dreams and endless hours comprise the endless day.

A year may be as wasted as a barren desert wide,
With nothing yet accomplished, and very little tried.

God, make my year of merit, one I may view with pride,
Help me spread a ray of sunshine in this world where I abide.

Help me to stay my brother's tear by word or deeds well meant,
Thus his burden may be lightened, and my year will be well spent.

THE GRAVEYARD OF MY DREAMS

My last fond dream, I sadly bid adieu,
Torn from my grasp by ethereal hands it seems,
To join the multitude decaying where
A phantom stalks the graveyard of my dreams.

One by one, I've watched them fade and die.
The echoes of each epitaph resound,
Orated by a spector stalking there,
Midst golden dreams that molder in the ground.

I glimpse a floating gown of gossamer,
I hear the banshee's mournful, wailing screams.
Why must my last small hope succumb before
I perish like my dear, departed dreams.

MY FIRST DAY OF SCHOOL

Marvel Schoolhouse 1935

'Twas early in the morning of a warm September day,
When I climbed on ole Machaco, and hastened on my way.
With a tablet and some pencils, stashed in a sugar sack,
And hanging from the saddle strings a lunch for noonday snack.

The three mile jaunt to Marvel, seemed like a lengthy trip,
Even though Machaco maintained a steady clip.
And when I had dismounted once more upon the ground,
I heard the school bell ringing, with a tinkling kind of sound.

And then I saw the children had stopped their game of tag,
And turning toward Old Glory, pledged allegiance to the flag.
As I marched into the school, I was a little bit uptight,
Thinking that a school kid, could surely read and write.

And since I could do neither, and had never been to school,
Being red-haired and left handed, they might take me for a fool.
I don't know what I learned that day, guess not enough to tell,
But I know if you were good, you got to ring the recess bell.

But if your name was posted for all the school to see,
Then you could get a couple marks, but better not get three.
I never learned the consequence of what those marks could do,
'Cause when my name was posted, I would always stop at two!

My first day at the Marvel school, in Nineteen-thirty-five
Foretold of many happy years, and dreams that stayed alive!

MARVEL

On a high and windswept mesa sleeping peacefully in the sun,
Lies a shabby little village, crumbling in oblivion.

There a stark and empty schoolhouse, silhouetted in the gloom,
Keeps a silent lonely vigil from each dark deserted room.
Still it holds a host of memories from that distant by-gone day,
When the school bell's urgent ringing called the children from their play.

Where once stood a bank and pool hall decked with vines and hollyhock,
There the tumble weeds are blowing on a now deserted block.
There too stood the friendly country store; the General Mercantile,
Where farmers brought their cream and eggs, and paused to chat awhile.

A little farther down the street a flaming forge bespoke
The crafts a local blacksmith wrought, midst flying sparks and smoke.
But many years have passed since then, now in the setting sun
Lies the little town of Marvel, crumbling in oblivion.

HOW LONG IS A MONTH?

They say a month is thirty days
(Though sometimes more or less.)
How long a time it really is
Depends on us, I guess.

It's length of time is altered by
The things it holds in store.
How long a month can be depends
On what you're waiting for.

They say a month is thirty days
(Give or take a few.)
It seems the rent has just been paid,
And now it's overdue.

That payday I've been looking for
Seems <u>never</u> to arrive!
There's only been four weeks this month?
Oh, come now, there's been five!

But, no, there must have just been <u>three,</u>
For now I recollect . . .
Payday I paid the paper boy
When he came to collect.

Then I recall that just last month
Vacation time was here . . .
It hasn't been just four short weeks!
I'm sure it's been a year.

They say a month is thirty days
(This thinking I deplore)!
How long a month can be depends
On what you're waiting for!

I AM MY BROTHER'S KEEPER

I am not my brother's keeper, is a saying old as time.
You'll hear it oft' repeated in a story or in a rhyme.
I hope you will remember, paper does not refuse ink,
As so many things you read will give you pause to stop and think.

For you are your brother's keeper, and the Bible tells us so,
To earn your way to heaven, seeds of kindness you must sow.
I don't think that God intended some should have and some should not,
If the Lord has truly blessed you, and you're one of those whose got,

Then you are your brother's keeper, God gave much that you can spare.
For when he gave you riches, He expected you to share.
First he filled your every need, and then he gave you more;
Likened to a mighty vessel, duty bound to reach the shore.

EVERYBODY'S GOTTA
BE SOMEWHERE

When I was but a barefoot lad, and should have been in school,
My teacher came upon me, down at the swimming pool.
A hickory stick was in his hand, He said, "What are you doing here?"
Well, everybody's gotta be somewhere.

As wedding bells were ringing out for me and Mary Lou,
I spied a face amongst the crowd, a girl that I once knew.
A tiny babe was in her arms, she said, "What are you doing here?"
Well, everybody's gotta be somewhere.

I dropped in on a friend of mine; she poured a drink of gin,
And things were getting cozy when her husband happened in.
A forty-five was in his hand, he said, "What are you doing here?"
Well, everybody's gotta be somewhere.

Now when I climb those golden stairs, and reach the pearly gate,
Saint Peter's gonna take one look, and this will be my fate,
With the golden rule book in his hand, he'll say, "What are you doing here?"
Well, everybody's gotta be somewhere!

BOWLING

I eagerly joined a bowling team,
For I held myself in high esteem.
I could run like a deer and dance with grace,
And nothing got by when I played first base.
And the rules allowed a handicap,
No doubt this bowling would be a snap.

By way of advice, I'm simply told
You don't look up 'til your ball is rolled.
You reach 'way out and follow through,
And your ball will do what a ball should do.
Though no two people bowl alike,
Just hit the pocket and make a strike.

I watched the mark as I rolled my ball.
I would not look up 'til the pins should fall . . .
Where is the clutter of falling pins?
They stand unmoved like mannequins.
As all is silent, not even a flutter,
For I'd rolled my ball straight down the gutter!

I tell myself it's all in the game,
And I'm sure to improve the following frame.
But my teammates watch with an anxious air
As I miss my mark and leave my spare!

And thus it goes from week to week,
And I trust my problem is not unique.
But one thing certain, that's not in the books:
It isn't as easy as it looks!

Ramona Cugnini

THE SONG OF THE
ANTIQUE COLLECTOR

There's nothing I've bought, that I wish I'd bought less,
And most times I wish I'd bought more.
The dealer is smiling and licking his chops,
Each time I walk through the door.

Glassware antique, painted china, I seek,
And all things from years that are passed.
I love this old stuff, and I can't get enough,
But I'm losing my bank account fast.

There's nothing I've bought that I wished I'd bought less,
And most times I wish I'd bought more.
So I'll cling to my treasures, and still I'll be rich,
When I'm homeless, hungry and poor.

THE SIGN READS "SOLD"

Oh little house, you've been my home,
My haven from the storm.
Within the comfort of your walls,
You've held me safe and warm.

The lush, green grass on which you rest,
The climbing rose of red,
The dainty, fragile columbine,
The budding tulip bed.

These things I now must bid adieu.
I'll go and not look back.
To seek once more your tranquil peace
In mansion or in shack.

Who knows which way my path will lead?
Who knows my destiny?
I bid farewell, my happy home.
May peace abide with thee.

CLOUDS

Today I watched the dark blue sky,
And saw the wispy clouds pass by.
I wondered why God put them there,
Those little puffs up in the air.

Some formed themselves in shapes of frogs,
Some looked like horses, some like dogs.
But soon their shapes were sure to change,
They looked like puffing dragons, strange.

I guess if clouds aren't going to rain,
They must be there to entertain.
For I had spent the livelong day,
Watching them come and go away.

TODAY

Don't dwell on the future, nor live in the past,
But look to the moment at hand.
For the deeds that are etched on the beach of today,
Will long leave their mark in the sand.

Remember the past, with it's moments of glory,
Have faith in tomorrow's acclaim,
But don't be content with yesterday's laurels,
Nor visions of fortune and fame.

For now is your day, and this is your hour.
Take care that it slips not away,
For soon comes the moment it will be the past,
And the future depends on today.

THE ODE TO THE FISHERMAN

Beside a muddy shallow stream, he sits day after day,
He's never had steady job, nor earned a steady pay.
He braves the cold and blazing sun; what does this strange man think?
I see so little water there and not a drop to drink.
And strangers passing down the road remark upon his fate.
They wonder if he has a hook, and what is used for bait.

They say when time permits them, they're gonna stop and chat,
And maybe leave a raincoat, or at least some kind of hat.
They fear that maybe sometime when they pass that barren stream,
The old man may not be there, given up upon his dream.
And days pass by and turn to months, and what to some seems strange,
He fishes in that same old creek, without a bit of change.

He dreams about the fish he'll catch and those that got away.
He's gonna catch the big one if it takes 'til Judgment Day!
So as you cast your fishing line out in life's rapid stream,
If the line is reeled in empty, hold tightly to your dream.
Be like our friend, the fisherman; don't quit and don't give in.
For the man who keeps on trying is the man whose gonna win.

HIGH-MINDED DREAMER

Some people might call him a high-minded dreamer.
Each spring he packs up and leaves.
His horses stand tied side by side in the trailer,
Down the highway he's pullin' his dreams.

He's up at the first crack of dawn in the morning,
Feeding and grooming his colts.
His wife keeps the warm home fires burning,
She knows he'll be driftin' back home.

That's how it goes for a high-minded dreamer,
Who follows his dream to the end.

He's hoping the season will bring him a winner,
If only one horse would succeed.
He's dreamin', just hopin' to have him a winner,
One horse with brilliance and speed.

The chances are good that someday he'll make it,
The trophy one day will be his,
If fightin' the odds to the end makes a winner,
There's no way that this dream can miss.

For that's how it goes for a high-minded dreamer,
Who follows his dream to the end.

MY HOPES

I wouldn't ask that every hand you hold's a winner.
I wouldn't ask you always get that lucky spin.
I only ask that when the cards pass 'round the table,
The dealer knows you've come to play, and deals you in.

If you believe the cards you hold to be a winner,
I hope you never throw away the winning hand.
I hope you don't give up on things that you believe in,
I hope they know you've come to play, and deal you in.

I hope you're strong enough to lose, and take your losses,
And if you're down, that you get up to fight again.
And that the best will know you've earned your place among them,
And they will know you've come to play, and deal you in.

IF I WERE A BREEZE

If I were a breeze, I would scurry away.
I'd skip through the meadow; I'd romp in the hay.

I'd chase the bright leaves that go scampering by.
You'd hear my sweet song in the pines gentle sigh.

I'd carry the notes that the meadow larks sing,
And the fragrance of flowers that blossom in spring.

To the presence of someone caught up in life's game,
Grown weary with seeking his fortune and fame.

Thus his cares would be lessened, his spirit made gay,
As the toil of a lifetime would vanish away.

But unlike the cool breeze that hastens away,
My roots go too deep, and it's here I will stay.

And my days will be bright, and my heart set at ease
By the gift that is borne on each soft, gentle breeze.

Ramona Cugnini

OUR COUNTRY

Be proud that you live in the U.S.A.
Be glad this land is ours,
And thank the lord in a humble way,
And salute the stripes and stars.

From California with it's redwood trees,
To the rockbound coast of Maine,
'cross the fertile valleys where the grass grows green,
'cross the gentle rolling plain.

There is Colorado, where the mountain peaks
Reach up to touch the sky,
And South Dakota where the granite speaks
Of men who will never die.

From the rich Ohio, where the golden corn
Is standing row on row,
To the western desert, where the cliffs adorn
The land of the Navajo.

From the Mississippi to the great Salt Lake,
From the south land to the shores,
Be glad that you live in the U.S.A.
Be proud this land is ours.

WHAT MAKES A MAN

Whether riding the white crest of public approval,
Or down on your luck like a bum in the street,
Don't fail to be humble for all your good fortune
Yet walk just as proud should you meet with defeat.

A man can't be judged by the hand that fate deals him.
His measure of worth is much greater, I'm sure.
In triumph, he must not lose sight of life's values.
In failure he must have the strength to endure.

So if Lady Luck has chosen to bless you,
Don't think you're a man of highest renown.
But should your endeavors lie crumbled in ruin,
Start building anew; let it not get you down.

UPON REACHING SIXTY-TWO

'Twas at an early age I learned
That one should leave no stone unturned.
And through the years I have been known
For turning over every stone.

I turned a milestone just today,
And there I found to my dismay
'Twas time to face the bitter truth,
I was no longer in my youth.

I've reached the age of sixty-two,
And should retire as many do,
But why quit now, while still so young,
There's many songs yet to be sung.

There's many hills left still to climb,
And many thoughts that need a rhyme.
There's many lessons still to learn,
And many bridges yet to burn.

It's now so clear I should have known
My folly when I turned that stone,
I guess you'd say that now I've learned
Some stones are better left unturned.

I turned that milestone back around,
And left it lying in the ground.
Perhaps, some day, I don't know when,
I'll ever turn that stone again!

THE APPLE DOESN'T FALL
FAR FROM THE TREE

A pretty wife, a little girl, two people who make up my world.
A happy man, oh lucky me, the apple doesn't fall far from the tree.

High school sweethearts, you and me, we talked of marriage soon to be,
Then came the day when all the town, beheld you in your wedding gown.

When to our lives a baby came, just like her mother she became,
Fashioned from a perfect mold, with smiling eye and heart of gold.

Our little girl will soon be grown, and start a family of her own.
The man is blessed whom she endows, when she repeats her wedding vows.

A pretty wife, a little girl, two people who make up my world.
A happy man, oh lucky me, the apple doesn't fall far from the tree.

AN "OLD ADAGE" STORY

(STRAIGHT FROM THE HORSES MOUTH)

You can lead a horse to water,
But you cannot make it drink,
Is something we have often heard.
That's what the old folks think.

And still water runs the deepest,
Maybe that's why he won't drink.
All things come to he who waits,
That's what they'd have you think.

But I've been waiting patiently,
Upon this river's brink.
You never spur a willing horse.
Just hope that he will drink!

I've heard that silence's golden,
So I'll just sit here and wait.
No use to lock the barn door now,
It seems a little late.

They say don't beat a dead horse,
And I fear he may have died.
I wish he'd seen the greener grass
That's on the other side.

But if wishes all were horses,
Then a beggar he might ride.
I'll set here 'neath this old oak tree,
From which an acorn grew.

To look a gift horse in the mouth,
Is one thing I'd not do!
Or change my horses in midstream;
I would not do that, too!

But all is well that ends well, Unless an ill wind blew!

ALL OF ONE SIZE

This world really isn't a bad place to live,
If you get your take, and it isn't all give,
If you've never had your high hopes dashed aground,
Or a dream taken from you before it was found.

When you get a yacht and a new Cadillac,
And your ice in a mounting, and not down your back.
If all your opinions conform to the pack,
If you're not an outcast, a dropout, or black.

And poverty only comes to a few,
Which isn't so bad, unless one of them's you.
No one was born booted, with bright shiny spurs,
To ride on my back, and neither on yours.
A truth that so many do not realize,
That plot in the ground, makes us all of one size.

A MODERN DAY "SANTA" MOM

For many years old Santa Claus arrived on Christmas Eve.
His sleigh piled high with dolls and sleds, and other toys to leave.
Pulled by his tiny reindeer, across the frozen sky,
While Mama cooked the turkey, and made the pumpkin pie.

But now it seems that Mama has taken Santa's chore,
Instead of dancing reindeer hooves, you'll hear that engine roar.
For Mama drives an SUV, as modern Santa's should,
She doesn't need the reindeer, just the horses 'neath the hood.

She doesn't fly across the sky, for all the world to see,
But Mama's going shopping, in her flying SUV.
By end of day she's headed home, her gifts all neatly sowed,
Her SUV is groaning under such a heavy load!

So Santa, rest your reindeers, put those jingle bells away,
For Mama has it covered for a Merry Christmas day!

A FAIRY TALE

One day and long ago,
lived a girl you'd like to know,
Who only lived to satisfy her mate.
She was young and she was pretty,
She was smart and she was witty,
She was never tired or stressed, and never late.

She was quiet and subdued,
Never loud and never rude,
The kind a man would like to meet some day.
But don't go out and seek
The girl of which I speak,
That was long ago, and only for a day!

GO FOR THE GOOD TIMES

I was broke, lost and lonely,
With lots of time for thinkin.'
Thinkin' of the many times
I'd finished next to last.

When a voice spoke and told me,
If you want to be a winner,
Gotta look to the future,
Gotta break with the past.

You've gotta go for the good times,
Forget all the bad times.
Don't let your failures
Become the only truth.

Don't rein in your horses,
As they try to clear the hurdles.
Spur them up and over,
Then offer no excuse.

You've gotta ride for the finish.
Gotta stay in the runnin.'
Gotta whip and gotta spur,
Until the race is through.

DON'T MAKE ME COME DOWN THERE

When I was young, I was so bad.
I'd sass my mom, and mock my dad.
And once when I was just a brat,
And teased the dog, and scared the cat,
A voice rang our both loud and clear,

"YOU BETTER NOT MAKE ME COME DOWN THERE!"

I got so good, I really tried.
For I knew he was on their side,
And every since, when I've been bad,
I hoped I hadn't made him mad,
For all my life I've had that fear,
That I would "MAKE HIM COME DOWN HERE."

LEGENDS

A TENDERFOOT AT MESA VERDE

I went to visit the Cliff Dweller's home,
Through sage and sand, and sticks and stone.
The path was long, the sun was hot,
A hiker and climber, I guess I'm not.

My nose was red from too much sun,
But I had to finish what I'd begun,
And I made it back to the lodge again,
I was nearly "give out", but I didn't "give in".

THE WHISTLE SPEAKS

Echoing down majestic slopes
The whistle speaks of dreams and hopes,
Of the pioneer souls that were here before,
And the by-gone days that will be no more.

From the mountain peaks blanketed deep in snow,
To the rippling streams in the vale below.
Thank God, as the whistle again resounds,
For the glory and beauty which here abounds!

THE CLIFF DWELLER'S HOME

The canyons and cliffs seem to echo a hymn,
Revering the dwellings tucked under the rim,
For protection from storm, wind and war-faring tribe,
And a measure of comfort no words can describe.

The hopes and the dreams that were laid with each stone,
Never knowing someday they'd be forced from their home.
Never knowing their work would be left on display,
For the pleasure of others to visit someday!

THE TRAIN RIDE

I bought a ticket to ride this train,
To Silverton, and then back again.
The trip was slow and the kids were fretting,
My back-side ached from too much setting.

The mountains, the streams and the clear blue sky,
Were missed, for the cinder in my eye.
I'm back at last, and covered with grime,
But I'd like to do it one more time!

MESA VERDE

Nestled in the shelter of the mesa's lofty rims,
Where dwelled the noble Indian, in his beads and moccasins,
Where now the whiteman visits, his imaginative mind
Takes him back into the ages to a distant by-gone time.

And he hears the warriors chanting, and he hears the distant drum,
He forgets the crowded city, with it's ever-busy hum.
And he feels the loss they suffered, in the peace that he has found,
And he asks his God to bless them, in their Happy Hunting Ground.

LYRICS

LYRICS

VICTIM

If I become a victim, you can put the blame on me.
I cannot be a victim, unless I let it be.
I will not be your victim; I'll put to rest my tears.
There really are no victims; there are only volunteers.

Volunteers, volunteers, there really are no victims.
There are only volunteers.

A victim isn't something that another makes of you.
One does not become a victim unless you wanted to.
I'll put myself back in control and dry my falling tears.
There really are no victims; there are only volunteers.

Volunteers, volunteers, there really are no victims.
There are only volunteers.

THE RICH MAN'S TABLE

I get the crumbs from a rich man's table.
She has his ring, I have a label.
She has a banquet, she has a feast.
She has the most, I have the least.

I get the crumbs from a rich man's table.
He comes to me only when he's able.
She has his child, his life to share,
I only get what he can spare.

I get the crumbs from a rich man's table.
He dresses her in silk and sable.
She's his mate; I'm his "Baby."
She gets a yes, I get a maybe.

I get the crumbs from a rich man's table.
My love story is a poor girl's fable,
But he comes to me only when he's able.
I get the crumbs from a rich man's table.

WHY COULDN'T THAT BE ME

She tosses her hair, With a confident air
Her spirit so young and so free,
You gaze with desire
Your heart's set afire,

OH, WHY COULDN'T THAT BE ME?

The band starts to play,
She glances your way,
I smile through my tears, still I see,
You're caught in her spell,
And not hiding it well,

OH, WHY COULDN'T THAT BE ME?

Her hand's on your arm,
You're allured by her charm,
You're dancing as close as can be.
I'm asking my heart
As my world falls apart,

OH, WHY COULDN'T THAT BE ME?

MYSTIC MOUNTAIN

Upon this Mystic Mountain Top
Where I am doomed to wonder,
I hear my true love calling me,
Calling me back yonder.

Upon this Mystic Mountain Top
Where dense, dark pines surround me,
I know she searches for me yet
Though she has never found me.

Upon this Mystic Mountain Top
A frozen star defies me.
I'm hopeful she will pass this way
E're swirling snows disguise me.

I think I hear her call my name,
But wailing winds deceive me,
Upon this Mystic Mountain Top
My cold grave will receive me.

LIGHTER SIDE

"THE OLD WOMEN WHO LIVED IN A SHOE"

As Might Have Been Written by
OLIVIER WENDELL HOLMER

Aye, tear her tattered insole out.
Long has it been worn through
By the tread of too many tiny feet
Since I rented this rundown shoe.

Oh, better that her shredded sole
Should sink beneath the sand . . .
Her "tongue" is out; her "eyes" are closed.
Her toe's no longer tanned.

Tie in a bow her broken lace.
Then go with no regrets.
The Landlord says the rent is due.
Let's leave her where she sets!

"LITTLE JACK HORNER"

As Might Have Been Written by
JOHN GREENLEAF WHITTIER

There by the schoolhouse down the road.
A ragged beggar's sunning.
While down Jack Horner's greedy face
The plum juice still is running.

Jack Horner, you're a naughty boy
To eat that pie alone,
With Ragged Beggar looking on
With neither crust nor bone!

'Twill serve you right to live and learn
How very, very few,
When all your pie is eaten,
Will share their pie with you!

"BO PEEP"

as might have been written by
OLIVER WENDELL HOLMES

They have christened her Bo Peep, with her little band of sheep,
And again her happy steps resound, as she skips across the ground
With her cane.

When she noticed they had strayed, she'd been sitting in the shade
Far too long.

And she shook her curly head, and unto herself she said,
"They are gone!"

Now her crook is in her hand, as she seeks that little band
In the vale.

And with troubled tear-filled eye, Little Bo Peep begins to cry,
For she fears each little sheep has lost it's tail.

I know it is a sin for me to sit and grin at her here,
As she sadly weeps and wails for sheep without their tails looks so queer.

When she found her band of sheep,
They were playing hide and seek in the vale.
And the band struck up a note,
And then they saw the goat had no tail!

Ramona Cugnini

"LITTLE BOY BLUE"

as might have been written by
EDGER ALLEN POE

Once upon a noonday dreary, Little Boy Blue was feeling weary,
So he laid down by the haystack in the shade.
While he nodded, deeply sleeping, suddenly the calves came leaping,
And the Mother Cows came creeping, creeping through the fertile glade.
They were careful lest they wake him, for he'd end their well-planned raid
With that silly horn he played.

And the little sheep came bleating; to the cornfield, they were fleeting,
And the silken, sad, uncertain rustling of each golden ear
Thrilled them, filled them with a fantastic hunger they had never felt before.
So that now to still their bleating Mother Sheep began entreating.
"Do not wake the boy who minds us; let's fill up before he finds us,
Or he'll blow that silly horn for evermore!"

But the boy who does the beeping, still is sleeping, still is sleeping.
And the crops have never looked so bad before.
And his eyes have all the seeming of a demon's that is dreaming,
And the havoc that is wrought he can't restore.
And I wonder if he'll know, when he sees that trampled row,
Or is he going to sleep for evermore!

"HUMPTY DUMPTY"

as might have been written by
RUDYARD KIPLING

'Ere's <u>to</u> you, 'Umpty Dumpty, you 'ave 'ad a nasty fall.
Our orders were to break you, so we shoved you off the wall.

So 'ere's <u>to</u> you, 'Umpty Dumpty, lying quiet where you fell.
The soldiers cannot mend you, for you bruk your sturdy shell.

So 'ere's <u>to</u> you, 'Umpty Dumpty, an' I hope you'll understand.'
You're a slightly scrambled omelet in a first-class fryin' pan.

Ramona Cugnini

THE THREE LITTLE KITTENS

as might have been written by
"Constance F. Woolson"

There were three little kittens, alone, Sir;
Their Mom had gone away . . .
Gone down to the barnyard
To catch the mice in the hay.

They lived under the log house, yonder,
Their Mom was a fearful foe
Of every little field mouse
Who lived in the broad corn row.

She had knitted them some mittens
That fit them ever so well . . .
How much they thought of their mittens
They couldn't begin to tell.

At once they heard a noise,
As they peeked from under the boards
They saw the moonlight gambler
Shuffling a deck of cards.

Leaning against the pasture bar
In vest and stripped pants . . .
Bright were his eyes, like live coals,
As he gave them a sideways glance.

He passed the cards amongst them,
And these unsuspecting kittens,
Holding straights and flushes
Anteed-up their mittens.

The little cats viewed with alarm
A Royal Flush so grand,
As the wicked moonlight gambler
Laid down his terrible hand.

When Mom came home in the evening
The moon was shining high.
Her kittens had lost their mittens,
And they began to cry.

She didn't scold; She too had erred,
And kept it under her hat . . .
What else can you expect of your kits,
when their dad was an ALLEY CAT?

Ramona Cugnini

"SING A SONG OF SIXPENSE"

as might have been written by
ALFRED LORD TENNYSON

Half a pie, half a pie, half a pie onward,
Who's going to eat this pie? All the world wondered.

Orders had been obeyed, was there a bird dismayed?
Not 'though each blackbird knew his days were numbered.

Theirs not to make reply, theirs not to reason why,
Theirs but to fill a pie, 'though someone had blundered.

Pie crust to right of them; Pie crust to left of them;
Pie crust on top of them, stuck to their plumes.

Thickened with Knox's jell, salted and peppered well;
Hot as the Kiss of Death, hot as the Hubs of Hell,

The big oven looms.

Then flapping each gravied wing, the birds begin to sing,
When set before the King.

When can their glory fade? Oh the sweet chorus they made;
All the world wondered.

Honor the song they sung; Honor the gravy flung . . .
Score them a hundred.

THE VILLAGE IDIOT

as might have been written by
HENRY WADSWORTH LONGFELLOW

Beneath a spreading chestnut horse
The Village Idiot stands.
By switching to and fro the tail
His sweaty brow he fans,
With those long and flowing strands.

And children coming home from school,
Detouring from their course,
With loud and boisterous laughter
Spooked that docile horse,
And saw the poor man "squash".

Thanks, thanks to thee, our stupid friend,
For the lesson thou hast taught . . . .
Thus never underneath a horse
Will I be prone to 'sot',
But I will seek a Chestnut Tree,
When I am tired and hot!

"DING DONG BELL"

as might have been written by
HENRY WADSWORTH LONGFELLOW

Listen my children, if you've not seen
The dastardly deeds of Tommy Green.
Listen to me, and I will tell,
How he threw poor pussycat down in the well.
And her cries were heard by Johnny Stout,
Who said, "Hark! Do I hear a Catamount?"

"They scream once if on land, and twice if in water . . .
That sounds like the cat of the farmer's daughter.
I love the fair maiden who sleeps in the hay,
But she'd never give me the time of day.
To win her heart I must be brave,
And save poor puss from a watery grave!"

So he runs to the well with stealthy tread;
To the oaken bucket overhead.
A moment only he feels the spell,
And he tells his sweetheart, "All is well."
He knew by her eyes aglow with light
That the fate of a kitten was with him that night.

You know the rest. In the books you've read,
How he brought poor pussycat back from the dead.
How his sweetheart cut him to the core
With these words that echo forevermore!
"You're the bravest boy I've ever seen,
But the love of my life is Tommy Green."

LARIATS

COWBOY HEROES

There's much that has been told about the taming of the West
Of the many stories written these old ballads tell it best.
If Little Joe the wrangler, hadn't ridden for the lead,
To turn that herd of cattle, in their reckless, wild stampede.

And between the streaks of lightening, Little Joe had not been seen,
As he and old Blue Rocket tumbled down the deep ravine.
And if young Billy Venero hadn't tried to save his Bess,
If he'd dodged those wild Apaches, she would not have loved him less.

And the same for Utah Carol, who saved his little friend,
By holding back the cattle, but he met his fatal end.
And that old red-roan cabello, mightn't sun fished quite so much,
If those rough and reckless cowboys would have used a kinder touch.

And those unbelieving cowpokes stayed around to watch the fun,
To see that city slicker, when he rode the Zebra Dun.
But if the Tumbling Tumbleweeds had blown a different route,
Then the writer and the poet, would have less to tell about.

If those three ill-fated hero's hadn't drawn their final breath,
Hadn't gone to meet their Maker, by an early tragic death,
If they'd tamed that Roan and Zebra Dun, I'd tell a different tale,
And they may have sung Ti Yippee Yi, along the Chisholm Trail.

HOW THE COWBOY
HAS CHANGED

Yesterday a cowboy would
ride the open range
Checkin' on the scanty grass, and
hopin' it had rained.

Checkin' on his cattle
As a lonely blackbird sings,
And takin' home a dogie
Tied on with saddle strings.

He'd mount the wildest mustang,
And he'd need a lot of luck,
To ride this snortin' critter
When he broke into a buck.

He chewed the best "tobaccy"
And he kept a little flask,
Prob'bly filled with moonshine,
Though you didn't dare to ask.

In his rundown boots and Levi's.
Bleached by the blazing sun,
And a badly battered Stetson,
And a scabbard held his gun.

But now he drives a dually,
And he's proud of it, of course,
And he never swings a lariat,
And doesn't own a horse.

With his baseball cap on backwards,
Scoutin' for those barrel queens,
With the finest kind of runnin' shoes,
And tight, designer jeans.

Oh, how that cowboy differs
From those of days gone by,
And I wouldn't say he's wrong
He's just a different kind of guy.

Ramona Cugnini

THE RANCHER MEETS GOD

God was in his office checking off his list.
He heard a knock on Heaven's door, of one whose name he'd missed.

God spoke out, and called his name; his voice was clear and loud.
"I have to check the records; have a seat there on that cloud.

It says here you're a rancher; you've been ranching all your life,
And had your share of bad times, and you've seen a lot of strife.

The clouds would hover over when you really needed rain
To help the scanty pasture and wet the growing grain.

The rain was sure to come, you knew, and torrents would abound,
But only when your hay was cut, and lying on the ground.

The calf crop had been down a bunch, in fact, you knew it would,
And that pricey bull you bought last year was never any good."

The pearly gate swung open wide; God's voice spoke clear and low.
He said, "Just come on in my friend; you've had your Hell below."

THE OLD BUCKBOARD

The old buckboard's seen better days.
And so I would suggest,
It's like the countless pioneers
Who came to tame the west.

And if that old buckboard could talk,
The stories it would tell
About their westward journey,
And the wagon train through Hell.

About the rationed water,
And their scanty stock of food,
And worry that their meager fare,
Would not last their hungry brood.

As the wagons formed a circle
'Twas their fortress for the fight,
As a tribe of Indian warriors
Often struck in dead of night.

Many times they were awakened
By the warring Indian's yell,
And they tended to their wounded
Who were lying where they fell.

But now the West is settled,
And the buckboard's seldom used,
So it sets there in the sunshine,
And takes a little snooze.

And if that old buckboard could talk,
'Twould tell us quite a lot,
Some things that it remembers,
Some are better left, forgot.

But now it dozes in the sun,
Each day may be it's last,
Still it sets there in it's glory . . ,
As an icon of the past.

MY CHOSEN PIECE OF LAND

I'd like to take a trip abroad and walk with kings and queens.
This is just a thought I have that lingers in my dreams.
I'd like to go to Malibu and bask upon the sand,
But I must tend the cattle on my chosen piece of land.

I'd like to go to Mexico and fish the ocean, blue,
Or join in a safari; there's so much I'd like to do,
Or maybe go to Vegas, and hold a winning hand,
But I must tend the cattle on my chosen piece of land.

Yes, I'd like to take a trip abroad and walk with kings and queens,
But I'm a lowly rancher and not man of means.
Still as I behold my chosen land, although I have no throne,
I feel I am a monarch with a kingdom of my own.

THE TEAM ROPER'S WIFE

Take off your hats to the roper's wife.
She doesn't have any easy life.
She's up at dawn to load the truck.
He'll win this go, with any luck.

He's runnin' behind, but should recoup,
If his partner doesn't miss his loop.
If the steer runs straight, if they don't break out,
He'll show 'em today what ropin's about!

She thinks of the reasons they shouldn't go.
The fence is down; they're predicting snow.
They should stay home and move the cattle,
But his heart is set on winnin' that saddle.

She thinks of the things she'd rather do,
But she's there for him 'cause her love is true.
The kids pile in; old Shep's in the back.
She checks to be sure they've loaded the tack.

It's a long, long day, and the time will drag.
The kids will tire and begin to nag.
Her back will ache from too much sitting,
But she loves to see the fun he's getting.

When the ropin's over, the sun will set.
She knows they wont be leavin' yet.
The teams gather 'round relivin' the day,
Still chasin' the steers that got away.

And those who lost, forget the saddle.
They'll go for the trailer next week at Datil.
And she's happy because she's part of the plan.
And she'll always love him, 'cause he's her MAN!

A PIECE OF HIS HIDE

The cowboys were many, and tough as a knot,
In the boys of the old Lazy Three,
But the toughest of men and just out of the pen,
Was the sharp-shootin' Rusty Magee.

One day this bold outlaw shouldered his gun,
And mounted his big, strappin' bay,
To town he did ride for a piece of the hide,
Of the horse-trader, Jessie Mc Kay,

Said Jessie," my friend, you have met a bad end,
Say goodbye to the old Lazy Three,
You've had your last sight of a star-studded night,
You low-lifin" Rusty Magee".

Spoke Rusty, "My lad, has life grown so bad,
That you're tryin' to end it today,
It's a big cryin' shame you have played your last game,
I'll help Satan haul you away."

The bets were all down, and the bar emptied out,
The cowboys were linin" the street.
They had come for the fun, and to cheer the top gun,
And see who stood last on his feet . . .

The gunshots rang out, Rusty cried, "I've been hit,
Please, God above hear my plea,"
But all that he got, was Jessie's last shot,
And that ended Rusty Magee.

Jessie's barmaid came by to dress up his wounds,
Expecting him kneeling to pray,
She got there in time to share the last wine,
With horse-trader Jessie McKay . . .

THE BARREL RACER

She's daddy's little princess, in case you haven't guessed,
And he buys for her a barrel horse, that's bred the very best.
And he sends it to a trainer, who's the best in all the land.
And he buys a special saddle, and I bet it cost a grand.

And she pulls up to the rodeo in such a fancy rig,
The cowgirls know this beauty queen, is from a different league.
For all the other racers just made do with they had,
Mounted on a ranch horse they borrowed from their dad.

When the rodeo was over, and the prizes handed out,
The girls all finished close enough, it left you with no doubt.
It's something in your inner soul that sets you from the rest.
And it's all in your performance, when they put you to the test.

COWPOKE POKER

A bunch of the boys were kickin' back, and playin' a game of cards.
The dealer dealt each man a hand, and gave them his regards.
Lefty bet right into Sam, who threw his hand away,
Slim sweat his cards, and took a peek, and said, "I came to play."

"I'll call your bet, and then I raise," he'd drawn another four.
But Lefty drew the King of Hearts to start this betting war.
Lefty showed the boys his hand, when all the chips were down,
Slim's smile then left his weathered face, and now he wore a frown.

When Lefty drew that King of Hearts, he'd made a Royal Flush
And over all the jokes and fun, there fell an eerie hush.
Slim pushes back his creaky chair, and takes a swig of grog,
Shows four fours and a six gun," Lefty says, "you lucky dog!!"

COUNTRY DANCES

I never had a sitter, even not when I was young.
If my parents couldn't take me, they would just postpone their fun.
Families stuck together; there was never any doubt,
You stayed at home to play your games, instead of going out.

And if we got the chance to go, 'twas to a country dance,
And we didn't go each Saturday, but when we got a chance.
And all the men would hang their hats upon a wooden peg
Then grab their girl, and hit the floor, they'd come to shake a leg!

The women sat on folding chairs, lined against the wall,
The men asked everyone to dance, until they'd danced them all.
And during intermission, they put cornmeal on the floor,
The kids would run and slide and skate until the break was o're.

And at the stroke of midnight, the couples formed a line.
They'd get some cake and coffee, and only spend a dime.
The kids all watched those coffee cups and when the lunch was through,
They grabbed them up and turned them in, to make a cent or two.

And once in every evening, a square dance they would call.
The men would choose their partners, and swing around the hall.
It was "all join hands and around you go,
meet your partner and do-si-do,

Like a chicken in the bread pan, peckin' out the dough,
Granny does your dog bite? No, child no!"
At the Grange hall or the school house, we learned our social graces
And be they ever humble, I would seek no other places.

A MOTHER COW—A RANCHERS FRIEND

The tender, new alfalfa, was damaged by the frost,
The oats are needing planted, but I can't afford the cost.
The pump is needing primin', The ditch is dry as dirt,
No rain is in the forecast, but a downpour wouldn't hurt.

The steers are in the feedlot, and they say the market's down,
And I have another load to ship, the grass is turning brown.
I think I'll ask my banker if he'll back me one more time,
And trust me with another loan, at one point over prime.

'Cause I'd like to buy some mother cows, as Papa always said,
"If things are going badly, and you're going in the red,
If you're sinking deeper in the hole, and can't turn things about,
Just grab a mother cow's tail, and she will pull you out."

A MESSAGE TO THE BRIDE

A cowboy is a special breed
He loves his kind of life.
It's sometimes hard to take that step
And claim himself a wife.

For a cowboy loves his freedom,
As he loves the open range,
And though he loves his woman,
He's not inclined to change.

He needs to brand the yearlings,
And put them our to grass,
And he heard about some mother cows,
He really couldn't pass.

So he gases up his pickup,
And leaves at crack of dawn,
Saying, "Don't wait up with dinner,
'cause it looks like I'll be gone."

Much of the happiness they'll share
Depends upon his mate,
She must be prepared to hurry,
Or to hurry up and wait.

If you trust and understand him,
And love him with your heart,
You couldn't have a better life
'til death do you depart.

So ready up your wagon,
And hitch it to a star,
For you may reach the silver moon,
Or somewhere just as far.

When sharing with a cowboy,
His love may be your wealth,
I know how rich your life can be,
I married one myself.

WHAT I REMEMBER

I remember the Belle of Kentucky,
The horse with the star in her head,
The story you asked me to tell you
Each night before going to bed.

I remember the days at the races
You couldn't have been over four,
You spent the whole day in the pickup,
Taking your nap on the floor.

You'd play in the back of the pickup,
with your trusty old dog by your side,
· You'd share with him hot dogs and burgers,
And he'd share your pain when you cried.

I remember the days of your childhood,
And when you were well in your teens.
You were running old Bay 'round the barrels,
Dressed up in your rhinestones and jeans,

I've so many mem'ries to treasure,
I've so many mem'ries of you,
I'll always remember the good times,
And hope you remember them too.

MY WIFE

I've got a wife who keeps the books; I don't have time for that!
I've gotta see if the pasture's good, and the steers are getting fat.

I've got to get the hay hauled in; it looks a lot like rain.
She's addin' up the feed yard bills and workin the cost of gain.

I'm buyin' me a ropin' horse, a classy little roan.
She's figuring if the money's there, or we need to take a loan.

She needs to hoe the garden; she's let the weeds get high.
And she'd better pick some cherries; I'd like a cherry pie.

I've got to bid on a set of steers; I've given them lots of thought.
I'll bid them what the market is and hope to get them bought.

I'm lookin' over the yearling colts, darn! I like their looks.
She's meeting with the I.R.S., They're auditing our books.

She's meeting with the banker, then up to the C.P.A.
To see if it's better to buy more cows, than it is to sell the hay.

She goes to church on Sunday (I give her a lot of guff.)
I say she'll have to get a job; she isn't busy enough.

But it's good to smell dinner cookin' as I sit in my easy chair,
And gettin' up each morning, and find clean socks to wear.

I think I'll keep her here at home, just doin' what women do.
Shucks, what if she isn't busy; she's here when the day is through.

PROFESSOR JOHN

I was ridin' herd one mornin' just at the crack of dawn.
When over on the other side, I spied Professor John.
I don't know where he got the name; he'd never been to school;
He had no education, but he was nobody's fool.

He could swing a wicked lariat and catch a calf each time,
And break the wildest mustangs and spin them on a dime.
Whether notching on an earmark, or drawing on a brand,
He did it like an artist with a strong and steady hand.

There was no task beneath him, he did what he must do,
He would gather up the firewood, or cook to feed the crew.
He liked his coffee strong and hot, his jerky lean and dry,
And when the work was over, he liked a swig of rye.

I rode towards the eastward, just to seek Professor John,
But when I reached the summit, the professor, he was gone.
No he hadn't faced a wild stampede; no Indians had attacked.
He didn't ride the Zebra Dun; he usually rode the black.

I came upon on ole Blackie with no Professor John.
And later down the dusty trail, I spied his lifeless form.
His gun was in its holster, his canteen, by his side,
He had gone to meet his maker across the great divide.

So I laid him 'cross the saddle, and then we headed back,
The lead rope on ole Blackie, I gave a little slack.
The years had overcome old John; I didn't question why,
For he'd gone to help his comrades at the round up in the sky.

FEEDLOT CATTLE

I made a little bundle
Feeding cattle in the lot,
Thanks to your expert guidance,
And your judgment when you bought.

And thanks to you for holding out
To get a better price,
And knowing what a beef should weigh,
Thanks for your sound advice.

In view of all you've done for me,
It's not enough, perhaps,
To save you just one cattle hide,
To make a pair of chaps.

But still you know the gratitude
With which this gift is given,
Not only for your help,
But for a heap of happy livin'!

GOD'S MASTERPIECE

When God set up his easel to paint the western sky,
To paint the brilliant rainbow and hang the moon on high,
He painted the wide blue yonder, and added the twinkling stars,
And scattered them through the universe, and made this beauty ours.

He then sketched in the graceful deer, the wily old coyote.
Then brightened up his masterpiece by giving it one more coat.
He painted the lofty pine trees and added a babbling brook,
But before he signed his handiwork, he gave it one last look.

Then he sees that his work is good, and he needs to send a man
To drink in all this beauty and fit in the master plan.
He thought of a few good choices, considered a few good men.
Since none of them fit his picture, he considered them all again.

Who better than the cowboy, who's akin to nature's grace,
To see the beauty there displayed, a gift from a holy place.
And so it is, the cowboy who rides the dusty trail,
Acclaims this heavenly picture that's drawn to God's own scale.

HOW THE COWBOY STANDS

As I was walking down the street,
An old cowpoke I chanced to meet.
He stopped to roll himself a smoke,
Which soon engulfed him like a cloak.

His face was tanned, his legs were bent,
I sidled up to this old gent,
I said, "I hope I don't seem rude,
But I'm an ignorant city dude.

What happens If your buckle slips,
Your belt ends up around your hips?
From all the horses you have rode,
I noticed that your legs are bowed.

But even so, you're standing tall,
And that's the mystery of it all."
He shot at me a sideways glance'
Then hitching up his denim pants,

He spoke to me, his face was stern,
Said," Son you've got a lot to learn,
How cowboys stand, you don't know beans,
It's all the starch that's in our jeans!"

A LEGEND IN HIS TIME

He was up before the crack of dawn
And in his pickup truck,
Heading to the pasture
Before the sun was up.

Mounted on his cow horse,
He rode his herd each day,
Scouting for a sick one,
Or looking for a stray.

He could swing a mighty lasso.
Was a cowboy; was a hand,
He not only was a cowboy,
but a top notch cattleman.

On any kind of cattle,
He knew what they would weigh.
He knew about condition,
And knew if they would pay.

He would sell Calcutta,
For he knew that auction spiel,
And even if you lost your bet,
He'd make you like your deal.

He could train a thoroughbred to run.
He was a man of style
Who could take a common sprinter
And make it go a mile.

He would play a game of poker,
Deal a hand of twenty-one,
And pick a horse from off the form,
And know where it should run.

He was not a man of pretense.
You knew just where you stood.
He was always there to lend a hand
When for the common good.

And if the path was rocky,
He'd never fall behind.
There was no other like him,
A legend in his time!

MY DADDY'S STETSON HAT

My Daddy was a humble man, a man of little means,
Who always wore a faded shirt and pair of denim jeans.
His boots were worn, his jacket torn, his wallet usually flat,
But he walked a little prouder when he wore his Stetson hat.

My Dad could swing a lariat, could tie and brand a calf.
To me he was a hero, though he signed no autograph.
My Dad could ride a bronco, he was glued there where he sat,
But he rode a little prouder when he wore his Stetson hat.

And now that Daddy's left us his memory remains,
For he guided those who loved him with gentle, loving reins.
Now he corrals those shooting stars, and brands them where he's at,
And I walk a little prouder, when I wear his Stetson hat.

MY MAMMA

My Mamma was a doer; no grass grew at her feet.
She worked alongside Daddy to help her family eat.
My Mom could cook a dinner to feed a branding crew,
And she would make it all from scratch like women used to do.

My mom would gather cattle from the canyons far and wide
While mounted on a bronco that most cowboys couldn't ride.
She loved a verse of poetry, a painting of the West.
Of the many things she treasured, she loved her family best.

Now that Mamma's left us, her memory remains.
I know she's helping Daddy gather comets from the range.
And I hear their joyous laughter; they are happy where they're at,
And I know she wears a halo, and he wears a Stetson hat.

BIOGRAPHY

Ramona Cugnini was born in Marvel, Colorado on July II, 1929

Attended school at Marvel through the first eleven years, and graduated from Farmington, New Mexico in 1947. In 1972 Ramona married well-known cattleman, Patrick Cugnini, who passed away in May 2012. Today she still writes poetry in their home in Durango, Colorado.

OVERVIEW

This poetry has been in the making for over fifty years and covers most of the eighty-four years of the poet's life. She writes about love and life in general, and takes you into cowboy country where she has spent her entire life. The diversity of this book has something for all interests.

It touches on many aspects of love and life, with some humor, and shows the reader the history of life as the cowboy lived it. Mesa Verde National Park, as well as the Durango-Silverton narrow gauge train are also legends mentioned here.

The section, Lighter Side, reflects the imagination of the author. When you see this approach, you might find yourself writing your own nursery rhymes. Enjoy!

Printed in the United States
by Baker & Taylor Publisher Services